Embracing Your Spiritual Path

CONFRONTING DEPRESSION TO STOP SUICIDE

Andrew's Story

I0200893

A Conversation with
PHILIP BURLEY

Mastery Press

Phoenix, Arizona

ISBN: 978-1-883389-21-5

Printed in the United States of America

Philip Burley portrait by Images by Kay
Scottsdale, Arizona

Cover and interior design by 1106 Design
Phoenix, Arizona

Embracing Your Spiritual Path

CONFRONTING DEPRESSION TO STOP SUICIDE

Andrew's Story

A Conversation with
PHILIP BURLEY

Also from Mastery Press:

Mastery Press

Caring for a Loved One with Dementia
The Power of Self Awareness
Love Knows No End
The Blue Island
Beyond Titanic—Voyage into Spirit
Heart's Healing
The Spirit World, Where Love Reigns Supreme
The Hum of Heaven
The Wisdom of Saint Germain
The Gift of Mediumship
Awaken the Sleeping Giant
A Legacy of Love, Volume One:
The Return to Mount Shasta and Beyond
To Master Self is to Master Life
A Wanderer in the Spirit Lands

DEDICATION

....

To all who suffer from emotional and mental challenges: You are not alone—you never have been, and you never will be. Unseen loving spiritual beings who understand you completely are walking with you to guide, comfort, and uplift you in your times of greatest need throughout your life. As a professional spiritual medium, I work with people who are dealing with every imaginable kind of problem, and I repeatedly see the fulfillment of these words: "Man's extremity is God's opportunity."[1]

[1] John Flavel, 1627–1691

ACKNOWLEDGMENTS

Many thanks to Andrew, whose story is the subject of this book. His earnest examination of his reasons to go on living will go a long way toward helping others to make positive choices when they stand at major crossroads in their lives.

CONTENTS

INTRODUCTION

······································

Just two weeks before I met Andrew[2], a college student in his early twenties, he had attempted to end his life by taking an overdose of sleeping pills. He had a near-death experience while he was being treated in the hospital and had asked to see me after a friend told him about my work as a spiritual medium.

As part of my work, I have taught meditation, given individual and group readings, and provided intuitive counseling for more than twenty-five years, and I always allow my words to flow based on the guidance I receive to meet the specific needs of each person. After counseling a number of people who have attempted to end their lives, I know that a *negative self-image* is

[2] Names and details have been changed to protect the privacy of persons involved.

often the motivation for such action. The goal is just to stop the pain of existing. I felt great compassion for Andrew and wanted to do what I could to help him see himself in a new light, so I was looking forward to meeting him. I was eager to offer my support as he sorted through the dramatic events that so recently had taken place.

I had no preconceptions about how our meeting should go, and I saw my role as simply facilitating Andrew's telling of his own story so that he could hear it for himself and experience greater understanding of all that had happened. I wasn't sure how I could help him resolve the problems that had driven him to attempt suicide, but I knew my unique contribution would be to bring in the guidance of the spirit world and God in helping him see his own story from a loving point of view.

When he arrived at my home, Andrew was quite composed. Though he expressed frustration with events and relationships of the past and present, he was also trying to make decisions about his future. I learned that he had been devastated by a breakup with his girlfriend, but since his recent suicide attempt, he was struggling to put this bitter disappointment into perspective. My first goal was to listen to Andrew until he felt he had shared his story fully.

I felt that the best way to then proceed was to help Andrew anchor his sense of self-worth not in any relationship but in himself and in the saintly powers that have served all of the people of Mother Earth for millennia. Toward this end, I shared examples in my own life and in the lives of others to show how God and the spirit world intervene to shepherd us through our most challenging circumstances. If he could become more aware of his own spirit guides and teachers and embrace their reality, I knew he would be able to turn to higher sources for guidance about any problem throughout the rest of his life. He would also be able to better see and accept a realistic, loving, and positive image of himself.

Marked changes took place in Andrew's expression as we talked about the spirit world, spiritual experience, and the positive influence of spirit on our life's journey. Before my eyes, he seemed to absorb a greater awareness of his own nature as a spiritual being, find a higher vision of himself, and open his heart and mind to a new direction for his life. As we discussed his plans for the future, he was able to identify substantial reasons to believe in himself and live out his life on earth.

No human being is without emotional turmoil at some time in life, so Andrew's story is one we can all relate to. It is the story of a fellow human being who is heroically coping with despair that led him to attempt suicide; someone who is experiencing new hope through a growing awareness of the light and love that have always surrounded him. As you read Andrew's story, may you find a renewed sense of the spiritual resources that are within and around you, a firmer determination to grow through all of your experiences—however challenging—and a greater recognition of the unique value of your precious God-given life on earth.

—*Philip Burley*

NOTE ON DEPRESSION AND SUICIDE

In March 2012, The Centers for Disease Control and Prevention (CDC) published a report indicating that an estimated 1 in 10 U.S. adults report experiencing major or "other" depression.[3] Suicide has been cited as the tenth leading cause of death in the United States[4] and the second leading cause of death among college students.[5]

There are many degrees of depression with potentially multiple and complex causes and symptoms, including reactions to life events and biochemical factors; therefore, a qualified

[3] http://www.cdc.gov/features/dsdepression/index.html

[4] http://www.nimh.nih.gov/statistics/3AGES185.shtml

[5] http://www.pbs.org/wnet/cryforhelp/episodes/resources/sobering-statistics/12/

medical or mental health professional is in the best position to assess each person's situation and needs with regard to diagnosis and treatment. If you or someone you love is suffering from symptoms of depression or from suicidal thoughts, your primary care physician can refer you to an appropriate health care professional.

SELF-REFLECTION

Philip Burley (PB): How do you feel about coming here to meet with me?

Andrew: I wanted to come because I have so many questions about life and life after death. I thought you could help me find a larger perspective about what I've been going through.

PB: I want to hear everything about your recent experiences, but first I want to know if you can see yourself as having a future. When you think about that, what do you see yourself doing? What would be the most fulfilling for you?

Andrew: I'm majoring in English literature, because I like it, but I'm not sure it will lead to a job that will support me.

PB: Have you thought about teaching, editing, or writing?

Andrew: Unfortunately, teachers aren't paid very well, and editing and writing are fields that are hard to break into.

PB: English literature is a good foundation for higher studies and for communication of all kinds. So what other options are there for you?

Andrew: I've thought of going on to graduate school in English so I could teach at the college level or even going to law school, but I don't have to decide for a while.

PB: How well are you doing with your studies? Is it fairly easy for you to make good grades?

Andrew: I wasn't having a problem until I lost Gail. But after she broke up with me studying has been the furthest thing from my mind. I was so glad when the semester ended because I could hardly drag myself to class.

PB: I think one of the things causing you trouble is that you have depended on being with your girl-friend to feel good. When we're young, romantic love can be very addictive and make us literally high. Perhaps it's part of the grand design that we feel that way, but there's the danger of being very hurt when things don't work out. We literally "crash," and lose our sense of well-being and self-worth. It may also be a characteristic of yours to be generally too trusting or dependent on the opinion of others with regard to how you see yourself. I don't know.

Andrew: I think that's probably true of me.

PB: Well, it's true of many, especially when we're young.

It must be hard for you to think you can have a lasting relationship in the future because you have been so hurt in this relationship.

Andrew: Yes. I wonder about that, because I can't imagine being with any other girl.

PB: I understand.

Andrew: I feel like it will be a long time before I can see anyone taking Gail's place because I'm still very much in love with her. I don't see how I can trust someone else after what I've been through.

PB: Turn that around and ask, "Can I trust me?" Trusting someone else to love you truly is not nearly as important as gaining self-confidence and self-understanding at this point. Once you can trust yourself to love yourself consistently and truly, you will be in a better position to decide how to trust others. How do you feel about yourself?

Andrew: I don't feel worth anything at all right now.

PB: Did you feel different about yourself years ago?

Andrew: No. I never felt very good about myself. I think having Gail in my life is what made me feel I was worth something, almost for the first time.

PB: Why do you think that is?

Andrew: I don't know. My parents were pretty fair to me, so I can't complain. But sometimes they didn't seem to have much confidence in themselves either. And if that's true, they really didn't have a way to give me a sense of self-confidence.

PB: Did you have any siblings?

Andrew: I have a sister, but she is six years older and very different from me; we haven't been very close.

PB: How are you different?

Andrew: She is very social, and she has always been surrounded by friends. I have been much more of a loner until I met Gail.

PB: Something we all engage in is "self-talk," and unfortunately it's often negative. For example, we may break something and call ourselves "stupid." If I asked you to close your eyes and describe how you see yourself right now, what would you say? More than describing how you see yourself, how do you feel about yourself?

Andrew: I despise myself. I hate the way I look, and I feel ugly inside as well as outside. I can't really explain it because I'm not sure it's logical. I feel really awkward socially, especially around my peers. Even if my complexion is clear, I always feel like I'm walking around with a big pimple on my face—one that attracts the attention of anyone I'm with. I feel like I stand out in a crowd, but not in a good way. I feel like everyone can tell how nervous I am just to be around anyone.

When I was with Gail I didn't feel that way. Being with her made me feel like I fit in. I felt proud to be with her because she is so smart and so beautiful.

PB: And have you ever seen a counselor to talk about some of these feelings? Or have you done anything to try to change the way you feel about yourself?

Andrew: I've never been to a therapist. Why should I pay someone to talk to when I should be able to talk to a friend?

PB: Well, it's important for you to realize that many people have gone through something similar to what you have been through, and talking to a professional counselor helped them to understand themselves better. It helped them to feel deeper compassion for themselves and greater empathy with others. Seeing a counselor helped them to achieve greater understanding of their own feelings, thoughts, and behaviors in relation to challenging times in their lives. Many say that, over time, the experience of being in counseling gives them a better ability to use their life experiences to make decisions more positively and realistically.

Andrew: Yes, I can see that. I know what I've been through can help me become more mature if I can learn to see it objectively.

PB: The point I want to make is that it's important for you to do whatever it takes to be able to turn everything around and begin to say, "I love myself just as I am" and work from there. You may have the idea that you should be different than you are, but that's probably not the case. You need to be able to tell yourself many times that you have value to yourself and others—not by lying to yourself but by being really objective.

When I asked you about your sister, your voice got stronger, and you really spoke up. But when we talk about you, you speak very softly and hesitantly. This tells me that you don't have a clear understanding about yourself.

Years ago, I worked with a woman with a diagnosis of anorexia nervosa who was being treated at the National Institutes of Health in Washington D.C. With her permission, I worked with her doctor to try to help her. Her self-image was distorted. She was so thin she looked like a concentration camp survivor, but when she looked in a mirror, she saw herself as fat. When she was ten or eleven, her brother had molested her and told her she would get pregnant if she told anyone. From then on, whenever she put on a little weight she thought she was becoming pregnant.

Because she had a genuine phobia about gaining weight, she developed the habit of throwing up each time she ate. The doctors said her internal organs were the size of a child's, even though she was in her thirties. She died at a relatively young age from her disease. While you don't have this problem, I shared this story to make the point that a negative self-image can be very harmful, and even life-threatening, if it's not turned around.

DECISION TO DIE

PB: I'm aware that you took an overdose of pills, and your friend said you just didn't know what else to do after your breakup. Was he correct?

Andrew: Pretty much so.

PB: And what does that tell you about how you see yourself?

Andrew: That I have no confidence in myself without Gail.

PB: No confidence. You weren't able to picture yourself as doing all right in the present or future, and you couldn't say to yourself, "I'll be okay. This pain is a passing thing, and I will overcome it as I have other things." Instead of being able to think that way, you said something like, "I've got to end my life because I can't stand feeling this way. I'm not capable of moving past this." Is that correct?

Andrew: Yes.

PB: Why didn't you call your parents, your sister, or your friend at that moment?

Andrew: I really don't know; probably because I was planning on dying, so there was no point in talking to anyone.

PB: Okay. You had reached that degree of unhappiness?

Andrew: Yes.

PB: Could you describe what led up to that? I'm going to get some tissues just in case you feel like crying. And don't be ashamed if you do. Is it okay to talk about this?

Andrew: Thanks. Yes, it's fine.

Andrew: Gail and I had been going together for two years, and we had been very serious for about a year. We were having more arguments lately, but I thought everything was ok. Then, about a month ago, she told me it was over. She said I was too possessive and controlling, and she felt like she couldn't be free to see her friends or just do something on her own. I told her I could change, but she said she had heard that from me before, and she didn't want to get her hopes up again.

After we broke up, I still called her to talk because she said we could still be friends; but then she told me to stop calling. I think that was because I kept getting upset and asking her to change her mind, so I guess she got tired of that. When she cut me off completely it felt like my world had come to an end. I couldn't see a reason to go on, so I took the whole bottle of my prescription sleeping pills and drank as much wine as I could get down before I passed out. My housemate found me and called 911. Gail didn't even come to see me or call, and I'm sure she heard about what happened. How cold is that?

PB: Why do you think she didn't get in touch?

Andrew: I guess it proves she really doesn't love me.

PB: Could it be that she didn't want you to think that she felt any responsibility for what you had done in trying to take your life? Or that she didn't want you to think she would get back together with you because of what you had done?

Andrew: Of course I feel in a way that she is responsible, because she is the exact reason why I took the pills; but on another level I know that people break up all the time without anybody trying to commit suicide. It's one thing to feel sad, angry, or depressed for a while, but it's another thing to do what I did. In some ways I feel embarrassed and ashamed about it.

    I just love her so much. There is no one else in the world like Gail.

PB: And love can blind us, can't it?

Andrew: Yes. I feel like Gail's not contacting me when I was in the hospital is really cold, and it makes me wonder if she ever really loved me. I wonder if I've been kidding myself in thinking that she felt the same way I did. If she did, how could she leave me?

PB: It has to be very painful to think that.

Andrew: We were planning to be married when we graduated.

PB: I didn't know that.

Andrew: How do you leave somebody that you say you love?

PB: I understand. It must have been devastating.

Andrew: If she had done the same thing I did, I would have gone to the hospital or her house every day, just to be with her. It just hurts that she didn't even call. Maybe I'll be okay eventually, but right now, I still keep asking, "Why didn't she call?"

PB: It might be better not to guess why she didn't contact you. It's her business rather than yours. Since you don't know what's really going on with her, you can't judge her actions.

You may have thought your attempt to take your life would be leverage to bring Gail back into your life, but you know now that this is not the case. And if she is not going to be in your life anymore, it might even be better for you that she didn't contact you. It helps you focus on you, and that's where your focus needs to be.

How are you getting along right now? Are you functioning?

Andrew: I just feel like I'm in a complete daze and don't know what to do with myself. I'm supposed to work in my uncle's company this summer, but I don't feel ready to go to work.

PB: You do understand that anyone in your situation might feel the same way. It's probably par for the course right now.

Andrew: Yes.

A REASON TO GO ON

PB: You reached a point where you pulled the rug out from under yourself, and you're now trying to find reasons why your life has value—sorting out why it's important to go on.

Andrew: I have asked myself why I'm still here. Maybe there is a reason I survived; and maybe I'll understand one day what my purpose is on earth.

PB: Well, just the fact that you are asking that question indicates that you will know the answer some day. And the more faith and trust you have in the principle that you're here because there's a purpose yet to be fulfilled, the closer you will be to finding out what your purpose is. Your life *does* have a purpose.

In my work as a medium I meet many people who have either attempted suicide, had an accident or illness that caused them to have a near-death experience, or something similar. At my fortieth class reunion, a classmate who knew I was a medium told me that many years ago he had undergone bypass surgery after a heart attack. He was hesitant to tell me what had happened to him at that time, but he wanted to talk to me about the spirit world. He went on to say, "When I had my surgery, the whole time I was on the operating table I was out of my body up near the ceiling, and there was an angel in the corner watching over me."

He told me he survived to marry and have a daughter when he was in his late fifties, and his daughter is the reason he stayed on earth. I met his wife when their daughter was ten years old, and having this daughter had given meaning to both their lives. Sometimes we don't even see our purpose while we're alive, but you can trust there always is one.

Instead of thinking, "I'm a failure; look what I did to myself," think that you are at a turning point, and things are going to look up from now on. And know you're not alone. If we don't self-destruct by taking pills, many of us sabotage ourselves over time with negative self-talk by repeatedly saying things like, "You dumb klutz... why did you trip over that?" or, "Why did you say that? You know better." But whatever happens to us helps us to meet our destiny and become who we were meant to be. Just as it was your destiny to have this experience, it's also your destiny to survive and go on—to fulfill something that perhaps you don't even know about yet. You can actually look at your suicide attempt as a stepping stone on your spiritual journey.

I have drawers full of letters from people who say that what I told them in a reading has happened. They now understand something about their lives they didn't before, and they are making progress. You will, too.

FORGIVENESS—THE PATH TO FREEDOM

PB: From what your friend told me, you have parents who genuinely care for you. I know everyone has good and bad points, and I'm sure you could tell me the downside of your relationship with your parents, but essentially, do you agree that they are good people?

Andrew: Yes, they are.

PB: The fact that they have been by your side and have stood with you shows that they are making a continuous effort on your behalf. They gave you birth, and they're going to continue to be there for you.

Can we talk about your relationship with your parents?

Andrew: Yes. It's fine to talk about it. It used to be very rocky, and we have fought a lot about petty things, but overall it's better now than it used to be.

PB: Can you give an example of something you fought over—things you wore, friends, girlfriends, or what?

Andrew: I really don't know where I came from because we're so different. We're on opposite sides in how we feel about politics, and they have never expressed much interest in literature or art. My father never talks about anything important with me, and my mother wants to know too much about my life. Also, whatever I tell her gets around to everyone in her circle of friends.

PB: Have you talked to her about this?

Andrew: Yes. I told her I didn't appreciate her talking about me. It seems just common sense to me that you don't tell the world I tried to kill myself. Why would you just bring that up in a normal conversation?

PB: Your point is well taken. Did she agree with you that she shouldn't be telling people your personal information?

Andrew: Yes. She even told me she would stop, but I know she won't.

PB: I understand. What do you like about your parents?

Andrew: I know they care about me. My father has never missed a day of work, and my mother was a stay-at-home-mom who kept the house really nice and made sure our clothes and rooms were organized. Dinner was always on the table at the same time every day, and all of this gave us a since of security, I think. My parents are generally hard-working and dependable.

PB: And is your father or your mother more objective about things?

Andrew: Probably my dad.

PB: My take on it, intuitively, is that you're more like your father than your mother. Your father is a math teacher?

Andrew: Yes. He has taught for twenty-five years. That's why I know how underpaid and overworked teachers are.

PB: He has to be pretty competent and pretty dependable to have done that.

My mother has been in the spirit world for many years. It took a great while to get over the pain our relationship with her caused in my life and in the life of my siblings, but I have come to appreciate that she was not a terrible person. She had nine children; so what do you do with nine children? At the end of the day you're pretty beaten down. More and more I appreciate that she gave me life. If it wasn't for her and my father, I wouldn't be here. And she did her best. So for that, I have eternal gratitude.

These things work themselves out eventually. Once, while I was giving a lecture about the spirit world and life after death to an audience of about forty people, I suddenly saw my mother standing about ten feet away from me. When she passed over she was about eighty-six, but she appeared very young and radiantly beautiful—just the light coming from her was so beautiful. She said, "I'm so proud of you!"

When my mother was on earth, no matter what I was ready to do, she would say, "You don't want to do that!" About my first girlfriend she said, "You don't want to be with her!" Whatever I did, it was not enough or not the right thing. She disapproved of everything I did, and that affected me profoundly. On a subconscious level, I felt like I must not be able to make good decisions. But her appearing to me that night really healed me. I was so affected by her presence and her words that I had to stop the meeting. I didn't tell my audience what she said to me, but I told them she was there. I got so choked up that I just had to stop speaking for about five minutes to regain my composure.

My mother spent her final days in a nursing home here in the Valley. One day my wife had been taking care of her for eight hours straight. Vivien was so tired that I said, "Honey, let's go home. My sisters will stay with her, and they'll call if something happens." When we were ready to leave, Vivien and my two sisters went out to the kitchen area of the nursing home, and I was alone with my mother. I knew she could hear me in spirit, even though she was in a coma, and I said, "Mother, I want to thank you for giving me life. I love you, and I'll see you on the other side." I kissed her on the forehead and left.

After we went home, we were so tired we went straight to bed and fell asleep right away, but when we had been asleep about fifteen minutes, the phone rang, and my sister said, "Philip, Mother passed away about ten minutes ago." I was tearful, but I was also happy that she could go when she did. My wife and I prayed that she would go to the light, and then we lay down and fell sound asleep again.

Soon I was awakened by a voice saying, "Philip!" And I sat bolt upright in my bed. When I looked, my mother and father were standing in spirit at the foot of my bed with their arms around each other. There was a beautiful yellow light behind them and love was just radiating from them. My mother said, "Tell all the children that we are together and we love them." Then the image of a heart came out from them over the bed. It started out between them and then just came out scintillating and sparkling with light. It was about four feet wide, hovering in front of me. Then it went back to where they were standing and everything faded from my sight. It was such a wonderful experience to know they were together and okay.

My mother had never understood my work while she was on earth. But the next night she came again and woke me up, appearing very somber. She said something like, "Philip, I didn't understand you when I was on earth, so I really have to ask you to forgive me. Please forgive me." I said, "Mother, it's okay." I could see just one tear going down her cheek, and I said, "I'm all right. Don't worry. Thank you." Then she disappeared.

I'm not telling you these stories to impress you but to let you know that eventually things do work out. The most important thing is to forgive; not for the sake of your mother, father, or ex-girlfriend, but for your own sake. You have to let go of the energy of anger, frustration, or resentment toward them and forgive them so you can be free. And forgive yourself, too. You're a human being who is trying to make it through what might seem like impossible odds to any of us. I mean, who asked to be here? Who asked to be born into the body that we were given?

Andrew: Right.

PB: When I was growing up, I thought I was a very homely person and didn't like myself. But when I was a freshman in high school, someone helped me understand that there were good things about me, and with that, my life totally changed. I began to see my value, and I walked with a new zip in my step. Today, many years later, I've been able to help thousands of people through my work as a medium and counselor. If God has accomplished this through me, God can accomplish much through you, too.

LEARNING TO
SOLVE PROBLEMS

PB: Where do you stand now in terms of getting therapy or taking a step like that?

Andrew: I'm still resisting the idea, but I know I should consider it. Of course they sent someone to see me in the hospital, and that person recommended ongoing therapy. They gave me a couple of names.

PB: How do you feel about going for therapy right now compared to how you have felt in the past?

Andrew: I still don't like the idea, but I'm more receptive than I was; probably because I know I can't go on the way I am.

PB: You don't like it because it's an admission of weakness or...?

Andrew: Yes. I'm sure that's it. It feels to me like I'm putting power over my thoughts or my life in the hands of a stranger. I'm just uncomfortable about doing that.

PB: There is no one in this world who can have power over your thoughts and feelings unless you give it to them. The purpose of effective therapy is to empower you—first by helping you talk through and understand your own situation, and second by helping you decide how you want to look at your life and where you want to go from here.

Are you experiencing discomfort in this conversation with me?

Andrew: No.

PB: Because...?

Andrew: I don't get a feeling that you're judging or analyzing me.

PB: Yes. But a therapist isn't there to judge either.

Andrew: I know that, but it just feels so awkward. It seems so unlikely that I'll be able to trust a perfect stranger with my private thoughts.

PB: Therapists are human and can make mistakes. But again, who is the important person to trust? It's not me; it's not the therapist, but...

Andrew: I know. I have to trust myself.

PB: And if you trust yourself, you'll know if you have the right therapist. If you don't, you'll make a change. If you do, you'll know the person you're working with can help you sort things out.

Andrew: Another problem I have, besides losing Gail, is that I don't really have a direction for the future. I don't know what I want to do when I graduate. I'll be a senior next year, but I'm not planning to take education courses or do an internship in teaching or anything, so I really won't be prepared for any job when I leave school. That will probably force me to decide about graduate school, and frankly I don't know where the money would come from for me to stay in school.

PB: Are there are some graduate programs where you can get a teaching assistantship or a research assistantship?

Andrew: Yes, but I don't know if I'll be able to get one of those. There are a couple of websites that I know about, and I guess I could search for a program with an assistantship or some kind of financial aid.

PB: I think it's important to just begin. Maybe this summer you'll have the time to really just focus on you—working for your uncle, seeing someone even for a short course of counseling, and searching for a graduate school that has a program that seems like a fit for you. Taking a first step will open up new options and opportunities for you, that will help you move forward. If you find you don't like the program or job you find at first, you can always change it. You may change directions a number of times over the course of your life.

I understand how that can happen because it happened to me. It took a long time for me to find a clear and lasting direction for my work life, and I didn't become a professional medium until I was forty-seven. I was doing well in life at that age, but I didn't feel adequate as a person. I knew I had a spiritual gift that had been with me since childhood, and I knew I needed to do something with it, but wasn't sure what. I was fortunate to have close friends who said, "Philip, you know you have a gift. We've seen it, and we think you need to do something with it rather than what you're doing now." At the time I was managing large construction projects, but my friends said, "We think you need to get into spiritual work." Their words really affected me, and that's when I finally found myself.

Something else that helped me is that I have kept a journal for more than forty years. I've written about my problems and recorded many prayers in my journals. Journaling can be as helpful as other kinds of therapy, and it has saved me.

There are multiple approaches to helping yourself, but I had to learn to be very honest and objective about myself and what I needed. You can benefit from doing the same thing and just go to therapy because it's something you need to do—not because you like it. It may give you the support you need to deal with your feelings about your breakup and take your next steps about school and work.

Going to the dentist is my least favorite thing to do on earth. I have a cavity right now that I have to take care of, but I keep putting it off. So now I have to be very objective and say to myself, "Philip, you know what's going to happen if you don't take care of that tooth, so just go!" It's important to see the truth of what you need and find out what's really going on.

It really *is* the truth that sets us free; not our stories, fantasies, or make-believe ideas about ourselves, but the truth. So I hope you will, out of self-love, give yourself the privilege of working with a therapist to find out more of your own truth. We're as effective in life as we are in problem solving, and the more problems we solve, the more confidence we have about ourselves. Being able to problem solve is a key to our success throughout our lives.

When I was living in Washington, DC, I taught a course on Prayer and Therapy based on a course taught by a minister at Redlands University in Southern California. In a two-year study, three groups of about thirty individuals each were selected to engage in solving ordinary problems. Individuals in one group dealt with their problems independently, those in another group just prayed about their problems, and those in the third group prayed and also received individual therapy. The individuals who prayed and also went to therapy showed the most progress in solving their problems and in learning problem-solving skills.

I've prayed since I was a child, and my life-long experiences have caused me to believe that there's a force, a reality, or a presence who hears my prayers and helps me. But I also know that I can work on a problem with another person or write about it to gain understanding, and that combination helps me.

FINDING GOD WITHIN

PB: Did you have any religious upbringing?

Andrew: My parents stopped going to church after my sister and I started college. I think they were going just so that we would go, because they thought it would help us be moral people.

PB: And are you still a churchgoer?

Andrew: No. I'm interested in religion and philosophy courses because I'm interested in ideas about life, but I only went to church because it's how I was raised. I was actually relieved to stop going once I came to the university. I'm drawn to Existentialism, but I can't identify with any religion.

PB: What are your thoughts about life after death?

Andrew: I used to think that human beings invented God because they didn't know what happened to them after they died and needed something to believe in while they were alive. I was very skeptical because I saw no proof that God exists or spirits exist. I thought it was possible but not certain that there was a God, so I guess I have been an agnostic ever since I was old enough to really think about these things.

PB: Yes, I can see that. What are your thoughts now?

Andrew: I really don't know what to think about God any more. I think we all must be part of something greater than us, but I just don't know what that is.

PB: Without going into a great deal of detail, my experience from childhood is that God is within you. You are the temple of God, and to love yourself is to love God. The more you allow unselfish or universal love to come from you to others, loving all people as yourself, the more the God presence within you comes out and the more you are empowered to be fully yourself. We don't have to use any religious terms to describe this, though many have. It's the same universal reality whatever you call it. We can simply call it unconditional love.

People can come to know God as reality whether or not they follow a particular religion. Religion is fine if it helps you on your spiritual journey, but it's not essential. When I was a child, Jesus woke me up some mornings and appeared by my bed, and I still see him frequently.

I was on radio for three years here in the Valley, and when you're doing the kind of work I do on radio, you have to be authentic or they'll take you off the air after the first day. The morning after 9/11, my radio show was scheduled for 10:00 AM and Jesus appeared by my bed, waking me up at about 5:00 AM. He said, "Philip, many people all over the United States are troubled about what has happened and don't know what to do. When you go on the radio show this morning, just tell people to pray for New York and America and to see their prayers coming down on New York like droplets of rain—droplets of love. That will help them." So when I went on the air that's what I told the audience—exactly what he told me to say. Many callers expressed their appreciation of this.

I don't think I'm great or good because Jesus appears to me; it's just part of who I am and what I do. For me, Jesus is an example both of unconditional love and of what I can become. Even when he lived on earth, he knew God was within him and he was empowered by that reality. He tried to get people to understand that God lives within each of us when he said, "I am in the Father and the Father in me; and I in you and you in me," or words to that effect.

So outside of any theological or religious point of view, I like to emphasize the spiritual reality, whether you call it God, goodness, unconditional love, or even self-empowerment—it's all the same. When you tap into that energy, and you can, that's when you find your real self, and your false ego drops away. You can more clearly see how your life should go against the reality of how your life is going now.

Andrew: Right. And the two aren't always the same.

PB: They often aren't. Many religious people I work with believe in God and Jesus in a very specific way. They have a story based on their particular belief system. But most of the great religious figures or spiritual teachers taught that in the end they simply surrendered, because they realized there was only one will.

I believe that we can be in contact with the spirit world whether we are close to death or not, and that our own psychology and beliefs will influence what we experience. After you tried to take your life, you said you had a near-death experience. Can you tell me about what happened in your case? And has your experience changed your views?

Andrew: Generally my experience was positive, but it was different from some of what I've read about near-death experiences. At first it felt like I was dreaming, and then I had a sense that I was awake and riding really fast on a train—almost faster than the speed of light. Then I got the idea that I was actually "riding" into my own death. I was afraid at first, but then I felt like I wanted to relax and let go, and I wasn't afraid any more. I started to feel peaceful and serene, like I was going to some kind of destination where I would be taken care of. I felt safe and comforted somehow. I knew I wasn't alone, even though I didn't see anyone else. It all happened really fast, but it was a vivid experience, and not one I'm likely to forget.

When I heard the doctor's voice, I tried mentally to push that voice away. It was as though someone was waking me up, and I didn't want to wake up. I tried to stay with the experience because I wanted to get to the destination to see what was waiting for me. I really wanted to be in the place I thought I was going; but the doctor kept calling my name, and I started to sense the light in my hospital room. The doctor's voice finally broke into the experience and interrupted it. I opened my eyes and found myself back in the hospital.

PB: However you want to interpret the experience you had, I would use it to adopt that sense that you are being shepherded ultimately to a good end. You are in God; God is in you, and your destination is God, all at the same time. You have been given the opportunity to turn your attention to finding out God's will for your life. This doesn't mean turning outward toward religion, but turning inward toward your inner self and asking the question again and again and again: What is God's will for my life? Does this help?

Andrew: Yes.

PB: How?

Andrew: You're giving me a lot to think about, and giving me ideas for how I can use what has happened to me instead of letting it defeat me.

PB: Yes. Because I have great conviction, based on my life experience, about what I'm telling you, it's not theory for me. It's not something I'm making up on the spot. I know what I'm saying is true because I'm literally a product of this kind of philosophy, and my wife is too.

In 2006 I had a very profound experience. I had been meditating regularly for many years, but this time I was taken out of my body and into a state of being in which I, as an individual, disappeared, and "Philip" wasn't there anymore. I became infinite light, infinite love, infinite power; and everything that was, was within me. In effect, I came to know that I AM God.

Again, this experience was not about me as an individual as much as it was an event that took me to a new understanding of reality. Each individual on earth is God, including you; but to experience this as reality requires going inward consistently to become increasingly aware of who you really are. If you think in these terms, you will come out of this period of your life *far* ahead of where you have ever been! You are very intelligent, and you can use your analytical abilities to think through all the possibilities. That's my conclusion based on my logical and intuitive conviction about you. How does it feel to think you can be empowered in this way?

Andrew: It's something I'm not familiar with, but I would like to be.

PB: Well, just think about it. And don't be afraid when you are alone within your own heart to just say, "Show me this," meaning how God is within you and how you are within God. Ask to experience your own unique self-empowerment. If you can have the spiritual experience of going on a train through some kind of energy into the spirit world, then you can have the experience of realizing your own self-empowerment.

Andrew: Overall, the experience I had in the hospital was positive for me.

PB: Good.

Andrew: I wasn't frightened by it, and I'm still not.

PB: Good. That says a lot about you. It tells me that you are able to put this experience into a broader perspective.

I read for a man who was a sniper for the Army in Vietnam, and he was brutally tortured in his mind by this when he came home. Spirit came through, spoke to him about the situation, and liberated him by helping him to be objective about his experience and put it into a larger perspective. He received a clear message that he had simply been doing his job for the sake of his country, and in the ultimate scheme of things, everything would turn out okay for him. We can use whatever happens to us to become a wiser and more compassionate person.

What is interesting to me is that I can see a brilliant light within each person I encounter—the soul light. It doesn't matter what someone has done with their life or what ups and downs they've experienced. Someone could be an alcoholic or a murderer, but the light within is still there at their core because it can't be touched, affected, or destroyed. The soul part of us is never touched because it's the God part of us. Jesus saw this light in himself and in those around him. And in 1 Corinthians, Paul asks, "Do you not know that you are the temple of God and that the Spirit of God dwells in you?" The soul light is an essential part of every human being.

Even in childhood, before I could understand it, I could see the soul light in others, and I intuitively knew the answers to many questions. I thought others would think I was acting precocious if at the age of four, five, or six, I said, "Mom, Dad, this is the answer," so I often kept my awareness to myself. But I knew.

As an option to consider, you might enjoy attending some of my meditation classes. I think it could really help you discover new levels of yourself that you didn't know existed. That's what happened to me when I started meditating.

Have you meditated before?

Andrew: No. I have friends who have, and they recommend it, so I'm not unreceptive to it.

PB: Well, I will give you a number to dial where you can listen to a recorded guided meditation if you choose to try that.

Andrew: Yes, I'd like to listen to it.

YOU ARE NOT YOUR THOUGHTS: HOW WE CHANGE

PB: If you could change anything in your life, what would it be?

Andrew: Of course I would still like to go back to the way things were with Gail, but I would also change my opinion of myself. There are lots of things I've done that I wish I hadn't, but...

PB: Welcome to the club!

Andrew: Exactly. I know things I've done have made me who I am, and sometimes I don't like the person I've become. So I know I need to change my thinking about myself.

PB: And drop your perfectionist idea of who you should be.

Andrew: Yes.

PB: Yes, I know. Me too. We go to the extreme to make other people happy while we're unhappy and to make sure others are satisfied when we're not. So you have to turn all that around and make sure first that you're happy. And don't do anything for anyone if it's not productive or positive for you too. Just learn to say *no,* and to ask the important questions of yourself.

Regarding your relationship, as your life is changing, ask to be guided to the person who is really for you and to be able to recognize who that is. If that's Gail, so be it. But right now it doesn't look that way. Do what you can to make room in your heart for someone else to be the one. Make your prayer for the right person your mantra and be open to people you meet, because God or no God, the universal law abides that what you put out is what you get back. As long as you put out negative energy about yourself, and you keep thinking negatively, that's what you're going to get back, you see.

Andrew: Right.

PB: And if you indiscriminately go toward relationships without investigation and objectivity, you will get the same results each time. You will be continually disappointed and caught in a vicious cycle. You have to watch your thoughts in terms of what you're putting out there about yourself. And you are not your thoughts. Did you know that?

Andrew: On some level, yes.

PB: The fact that you can see your thoughts and be aware of your thoughts is an indication that you are not your thoughts. They just rise up, and they are not you. As long as we think our thoughts are us, we listen to them as if they are the truth, but often they are not. In your relationship with your ex, there must have been things you thought were true about her that were not true. For example, you thought you could trust her to always be there for you, but you now know you couldn't.

Who is it that watches and observes your thoughts? The real you is the person observing, not the thoughts themselves. This means that you can change your thoughts or even tell them to get lost! Does that make any sense to you?

Andrew: It does. And nobody's ever really explained it in those terms before.

PB: Yes. Well, it was a revelation to me too. Years ago, even before I became a medium, I took a meditation class and I couldn't believe my mind! I'd never been in my mind like that. No one had ever said to me, "Get very silent, very quiet, breathe, follow your breath, and see where it leads you. Then watch your thoughts."

Andrew: Right.

PB: When I did it I was amazed at the power of my own mind: its creativity, beauty, and most of all, the fact that I was in charge of it. It was not in charge of me. I discovered that I could change my thinking.

Andrew: You see, so many times people have said to me, "You have to change your thinking. You have to think better of yourself." But no one has ever made the distinction between me and my thoughts that you just made or explained how I have the ability to change my thoughts based on that.

PB: I understand. It's hard to change our thoughts, especially the persistent ones, unless we learn how to observe and direct them. If we think we *are* our thoughts, we don't see a way to change them. But if you just watch your thoughts as they rise, you realize, "Oh, these thoughts are in my mind, but they are not who I AM. My earthly mind is really separate from my soul." The earthly mind is like a vehicle or bridge to deal with this physical world, just as the physical body is like a diving suit to a man under water. Through the suit, he can interact with the water while he is under it, but when he comes out of the water, he interacts with his surroundings without the diving suit.

While we're on the earth plane, we relate to this physical world and its denser vibration through this physical body and our five physical senses. But the real driving force or energy behind all of our life is our spirit. Most people are not in touch with the soul or spirit, but when you begin to conscientiously watch your thoughts, you begin to get in touch with your soul. You begin to know, "I am not my thinking."

Thoughts rise and fall, come and go. People sometimes experience unwelcome, strange, or random thoughts and ask themselves, "Why did I think that?" But the fact that they can ask themselves that question indicates that the thoughts did not come from them. Yes, they came from or through the earthly mind, but not from the real self—the divine mind.

Whenever you question yourself or feel down, know your thoughts are affecting you, but you are *not* your thoughts. Your thoughts are trying to draw you away from who you really are. That's what the ego-driven mind does. That's its job. If there is a devil, it's the mind, because it plays tricks on us.

MEDITATION AND OBJECTIVITY

PB: A shift takes place in human beings when they meditate, especially if they do it regularly. When I had been meditating for about twelve years, I visited a PhD whose specialty was testing brain wave frequencies. I wanted to know what she would see if she tested my brain wave frequencies, because I had learned that if you meditate enough, you'll stay mostly in the meditative state or alpha-theta brain wave frequency. Right now, you and I are in beta, which is somewhere around fourteen cycles per second or higher. Below fourteen cycles per second is alpha-theta, and delta is when you're so deeply asleep that you're almost dead! This person specialized in testing these frequencies.

I didn't tell her why I came, but she prepared me by placing wires on my head and fingers, and we both watched the electroencephalograph brain wave frequencies. After twenty minutes I asked, "What are you seeing? You haven't said anything for a while." I had kept quiet because I thought her silence must be part of the procedure. She said, "Well, I've tested a lot of people in my career, and your results are rare. Your brain wave frequency stays almost constantly in a state of meditation at the alpha-theta level." I was overjoyed, because the test verified how effective meditation can be. That's why I recommend it to everyone for greater peace, better sleep, greater self-control, and many other benefits.

Andrew: Yes; that would be good for me, because I don't sleep very well.

PB: You will sleep better and better.

Andrew: I hope so.

PB: Yes, you will, because you are going to grow through this experience if you stay in the position of being a man and don't go into the mode of feeling sorry for yourself or dependent on the opinion of others. When you came in you were more the little boy, but now your body language, expression, and everything about you reflects the man or adult that you are. You have to be aware of that. It's tempting to retreat into being more childish because we get more attention that way. All of us experience this.

Andrew: How so?

PB: Well, if we are more helpless, we'll get more help. But the adult woman or man is the person who says, "This is what I decided to do, and this is what I'm going to do from now on," or, "I'm confident that I can do this," or "I'm confident that I'll find the answers, even though I don't have them now," or "I'll work to find the answers, whatever it takes."

In my view, you are on an upward course, not a downward one. This experience was like a miniscule blip mark on the screen of a life that will last forever in eternity. Learn from it and stay with the adult man you are. Be present for yourself, watch yourself, and guide yourself without depending on anyone. Don't hold this recent experience over your own head. Even if you have failures in the future, don't hold them against yourself either. Failures happen to all of us, and they are not there to pull us down. From

God's point of view they happen so we can learn from them. That's all.

When one of our daughters was around three years old, she was walking around our house when she fell down on the sidewalk. She didn't know I was watching her, but I saw that she cut her knee. She wiped it off and then said to herself, "It's all right. You're going to be okay." Out of her own mouth she gave herself very positive support, even at that young age. I knew at that moment that she was going to be a very powerful person, and she went on to graduate from college with top honors. As a little child of three, she understood the dynamics of self-support and self-approval, and she didn't come running to us or cry one tear. I found that I had tears in my eyes as I thought, "She has more strength than I have."

Andrew: My mother told me that I was never afraid of hurting myself when I played. She said my sister didn't want her to let go of the bicycle when she was learning to ride her bike, but I just pulled away from her and pedaled as fast as I could. I kept falling over and got all kinds of bumps and scrapes, but I kept getting up and trying again. My mother said I just laughed when I fell over and jumped right back on the bike. She was afraid I would really hurt myself, but I didn't worry about it. I just wanted to ride my bike. I don't know if I was being stupid or determined, but I didn't let the crashes keep me down.

PB: You didn't complain about getting hurt when you fell over...

Andrew: No. But it has always been that way for me when I get a bruise, a cut, or a bump on the head. I don't seem to mind it that much. I can feel the pain when something like that happens, but I don't seem to mind it that much.

PB: If I were you, I would bring that back to my mind many times during these days and draw strength from it. You will get up and go on after this, just like you did when you were learning to ride your bike.

Andrew: I know.

PB: Yes. You'll get through this.

When I look back at the things I went through as a young adult, I realize that I also confronted many things, including a period of time with the U.S. Army in Korea. What I was experiencing seemed very challenging at the time, but I lived through it. Life itself teaches us. Life is God and God is life. The most important thing we can do is to consciously decide that we are not going to go backwards by dwelling in the past, and that we will look at everything that happens to us as a stepping stone by learning from it and using it positively for ourselves. It doesn't matter what anyone else thinks.

Andrew: Right.

TIME TO HEAL

PB: Before we end, what questions do you have?

Andrew: Well, I could ask questions like, "Where is my life headed?" or "What's going to happen to me?" But I'm beginning to believe there's a reason I'm still here, and it will manifest itself in time. So I guess I don't really need to know if or when there is going to be somebody else in my life... or if I am going to go on to graduate school. I don't think I need to ask those questions. I just think I need to figure it all out for myself.

PB: Give yourself time to really search within yourself more than you have before, so if you can, avail yourself of therapy. A good therapist will put the responsibility back in your hands and help you help yourself. A therapist won't do the work for you, and that's the most important thing. If you encounter someone who tries to make you do what they think you should do, then move on, because such a person is pushing their own agenda. The only agenda should be helping you to understand what you want to do and how to take positive action steps to achieve your own goals. That's what it's really all about. Whatever the methodology, it should give you feedback that results in bringing you out of yourself so you can look at yourself most objectively.

Some therapists don't give any feedback but just look at the clock and say, "Well we've been here for an hour, so I'll see you next week. Thank you for coming." Then you pay your fee and go. Some give you very objective feedback. You have to decide what style or methodology works for you, but don't use style as an excuse not to see a good therapist.

When someone is sure that no therapist can help them, my guess is that it's because they don't really want to know the truth, or it's not their time to know the truth. They continue to suffer until they say, "I give up—enough! I don't know the answers. Help me." Then they become open to changing.

It's really true that no man is an island, and that's why I said, "Welcome to the club." No one is free of the need to break out of a situation or attitude that is preventing them from moving forward. I know you have the capacity for self-honesty and for directing your thoughts rather than letting them direct you.

Please keep in touch and let me know how things are going for you.

Andrew: I will. Thank you.

Mastery
Press

Phoenix, Arizona

For general inquiries send an email to
PB@PhilipBurley.com, or write to:

Adventures in Mastery, LLC (AIM)
P.O. Box 43548
Phoenix, AZ 85080

For more information about Philip Burley
and the work of
Adventures in Mastery, LLC,
please visit this website:
www.PhilipBurley.com

www.ingramcontent.com/pod-product-compliance
Lightning Source LLC
Chambersburg PA
CBHW021218020426
42331CB00003B/359